15
Fun and Easy Games
for Young Learners
MATH

Reproducible, Easy-to-Play Learning Games
That Help Kids Build Essential Math Skills

BY SUSAN JULIO

SCHOLASTIC
PROFESSIONAL BOOKS

NEW YORK • TORONTO • LONDON • AUCKLAND • SYDNEY
• MEXICO CITY • NEW DELHI • HONG KONG • BUENOS AIRES

Cover and interior design by Susan Kass
Illustrations by Teresa Anderko

ISBN 0-439-20256-6
Copyright © 2001 by Susan Julio
All rights reserved.
Printed in the U.S.A.

Table of Contents

About This Book

Everyone enjoys learning when fun is involved. And the best way to make learning fun is to teach using games. This book features exciting, easy-to-make, and easy-to-play games that reinforce specific math skills in young learners. Plus, all the games are designed to help you meet the new NCTM standards. Each math learning game identifies the NCTM standard and skill being reinforced, suggests the number of players, states the objective, lists the materials needed, provides easy-to-follow directions on how to play the game, and offers a variation for expanded game use.

How to Use This Book

Inside this book, you'll find reproducible game boards, cards, number cubes, spinners, and markers. To ensure durability, photocopy the game pieces on card stock and laminate. To assemble the number cubes, cut along the dotted lines, then fold along the solid lines and glue where indicated.

Keep the pieces together in large, resealable bags or folders. Label the bag or folder with the name of the game, the skill it reinforces, the number of players, and the list of materials inside.

Introduce a new game to your class by playing with your students or assisting them as they play. You may want to make transparencies of the game board and/or game pieces to use with an overhead projector to demonstrate the game or play with the entire class. Consider sending games home to encourage parental involvement.

Who Goes First?

• **Games for 2 Players:** Encourage students to take turns going first or roll the number cube to determine who goes first.

• **Games for 2 or More Players:** Have students roll a number cube to determine who goes first, second, and so on.

Ship Shapes

NCTM Standard
Geometry

Skill
Recognizing two-dimensional shapes

Players
2 to 4

Object
To be the first player to color in all the shapes on the game card

Materials
- Ship Shape game card for each player (page 6)
- Spinner (page 7)
- Crayons for each player

How to Play

1. Players take turns spinning the spinner to determine which shape to color in their game cards. Each player can color in only one shape during his or her turn.

2. If a player spins a shape and all those shapes have already been colored in his or her game card, the player passes and the next player takes a turn.

3. The first player to color in all the shapes on his or her game card wins.

Variation:
Cut apart the shapes and spread them out on the table. Have players spin for pieces and assemble the shapes to form the sailboat on the game card.

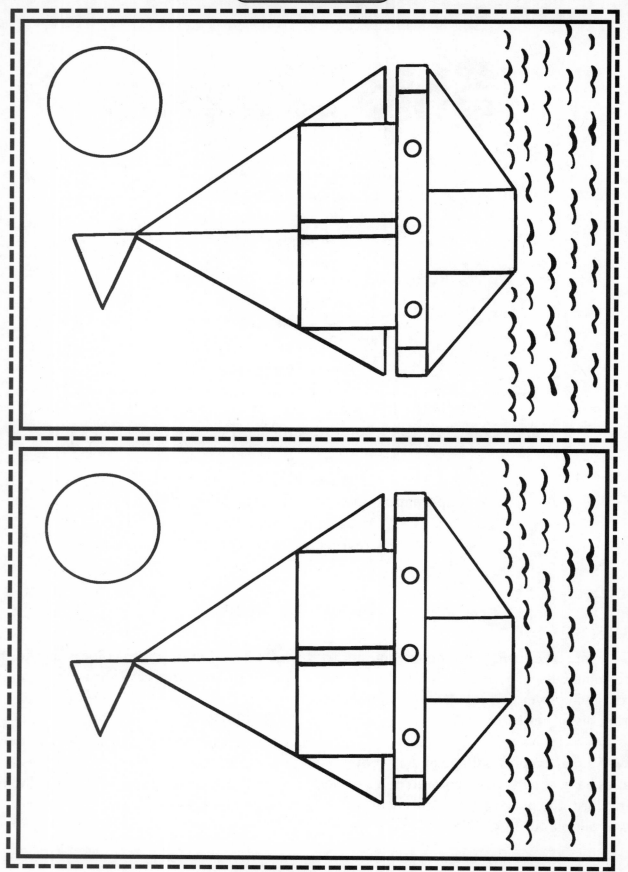

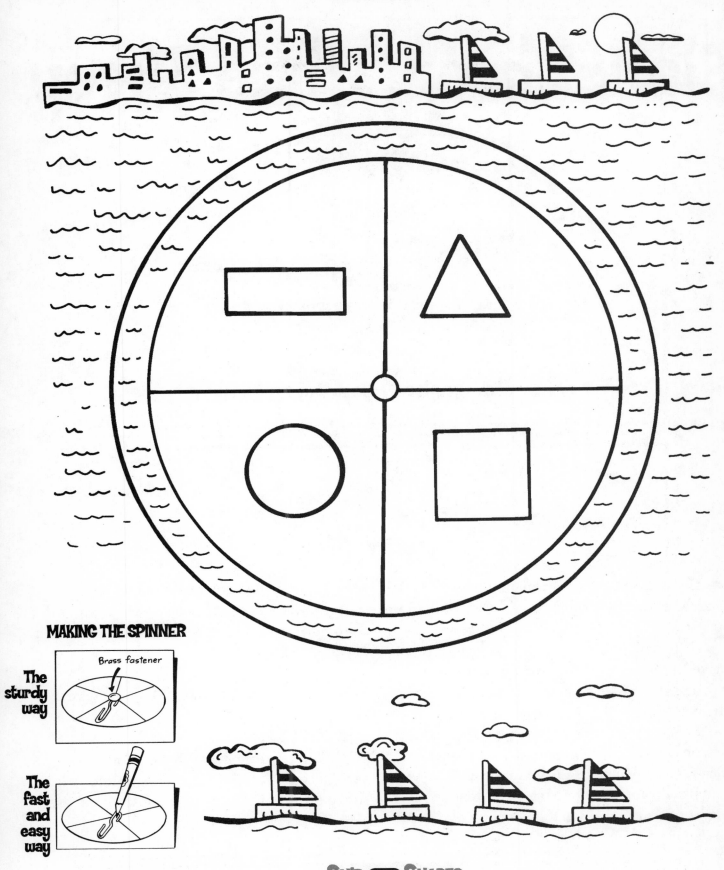

MAKING THE SPINNER

The sturdy way

Brass fastener

The fast and easy way

Black Sheep, White Sheep

NCTM Standard
Algebra

Skill
Recognizing and extending patterns

Players
2, plus a Scorekeeper

Object
To continue the pattern that the other player creates and be the first person to win 10 points

Materials
- 4 or more Sheep cards for each player (page 9)
- Paper and pencil (for the Scorekeeper)

How to Play

1. Give each player the same number of each black and white Sheep cards.

2. The first player arranges at least four of his or her Sheep cards to create a pattern. To win a point, the second player must continue the pattern that the first player started.

  For example: The first player could arrange his cards in the following order: black sheep, black sheep, white sheep, white sheep. The second player would have to place her cards after player one's cards in the following order: black sheep, black sheep, white sheep, white sheep.

3. If player two correctly follows the pattern, the Scorekeeper gives her one point. Both players take back their cards. The second player takes a turn.

4. The first player to get 10 points wins.

Variation:
To make the game more challenging, make several copies of the white sheep. Color the sheep different colors and have students use them to play the game again.

X Marks the Spot

NCTM Standard
Geometry

Skill
Describing and interpreting relative positions in space

Players
2 to 4

Object
To use clues to locate hidden treasure on the map
and accumulate the most Treasure cards

Materials
- X Marks the Spot game board (page 11)
- 15 Treasure cards (page 12)
- Crayons

How to Play

1. Shuffle and place the Treasure cards facedown next to the game board.

2. There's treasure hidden all over the island! To find the treasure, a player draws a Treasure card and reads the clue. The player marks an X on the board where he or she thinks the treasure is hidden. If all other players agree that the player has found the correct location, the player gets to keep the Treasure card. If not, the

player returns the Treasure card to the bottom of the stack. The next player takes a turn.

3. Play continues until all the Treasure cards have been drawn and collected. The player with the most cards wins.

Variation:
Have players create their own Treasure cards to use next time they play again.

X Marks the Spot

X
marks the spot . . .
on the rock.

X
marks the spot . . .
under the tree.

X
marks the spot . . .
in the swamp.

X
marks the spot . . .
**between the tree
and the rock.**

X
marks the spot . . .
**on top
of the tree.**

X
marks the spot . . .
above the rock.

X
marks the spot . . .
**to the left
of the seashell.**

X
marks the spot . . .
**to the right
of the seashell.**

X
marks the spot . . .
next to the bat.

X
marks the spot . . .
**over the
crocodile.**

X
marks the spot . . .
**below the
shipwreck.**

X
marks the spot . . .
**at the bottom
of the waterfall.**

X
marks the spot . . .
inside the cave.

X
marks the spot . . .
**at the top
of the volcano.**

X
marks the spot . . .
**beside
the dolphin.**

Cookies in the Cookie Jar

NCTM Standard
Number and Operations

Skill
Matching numerals to the quantities they represent

Players
2 to 4

Object
To match the quantity of chocolate chips in a cookie with the correct numeral on the game board and accumulate the most cookies

Materials
- Cookie Jar game board (page 14)
- Number cube (page 15)
- Choco-chip Cookie cards (page 15)
- Different colored buttons (for markers)

How to Play

1. Place the Choco-chip Cookie cards face-up at the center of the Cookie Jar game board.

2. Have each player choose a marker and place it on a START space. Each player should begin on a different space.

3. Players take turns rolling the number cube to determine how many spaces to move clockwise around the board. When a player lands on a number, he or she should look for the Cookie card with the same number of chocolate chips. If the player is correct, he or she gets to keep the Cookie.

4. Play continues around the board until all the cookies are gone. The player with the most cookies wins.

Variation:
Play "Backwards Cookie Jar." Deal Cookie cards to each player. Instead of collecting Cookie cards from the Cookie Jar, players try to get their Cookies back in the Jar.

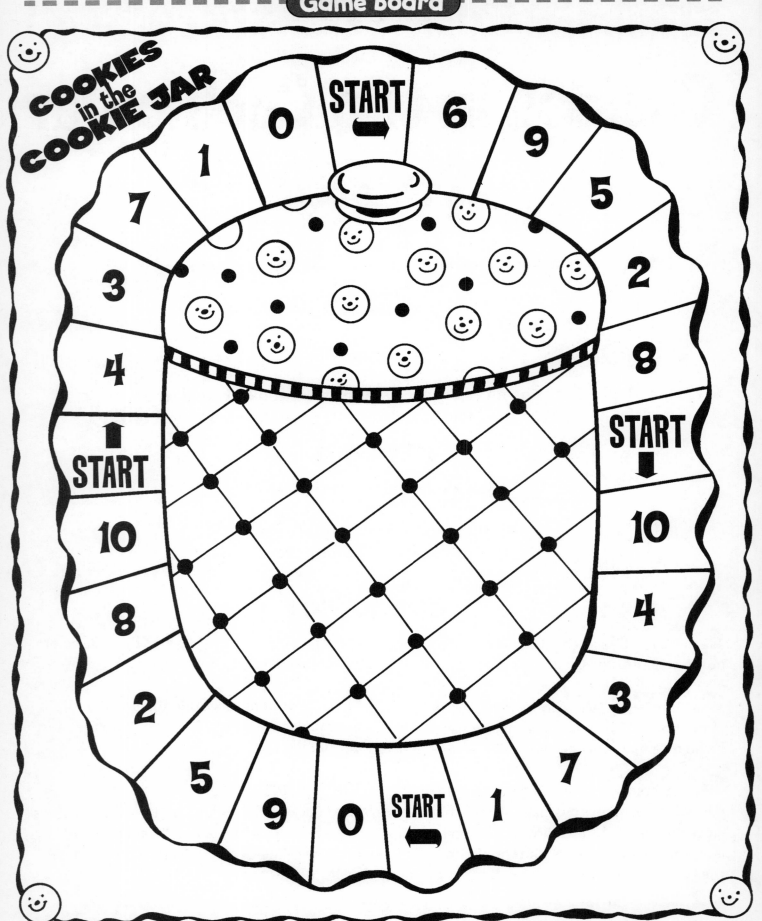

CHOCO-CHIP COOKIE CARDS

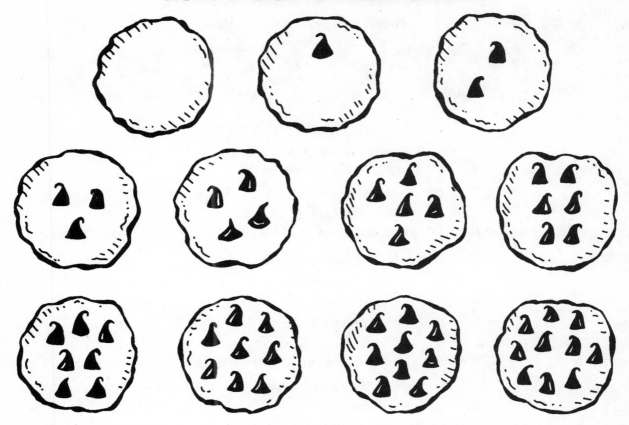

NUMBER CUBE

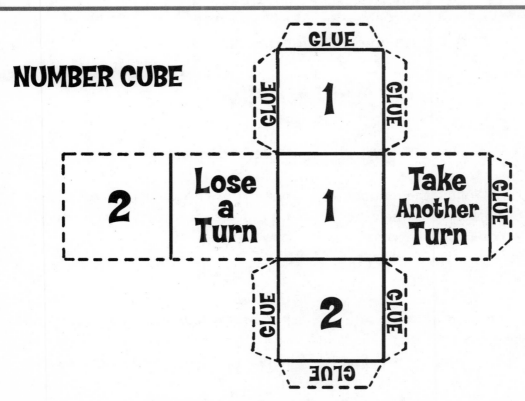

Shark Attack

NCTM Standard
Number and Operations

Skill
Understanding number relationships (greater than/less than/equal to)

Players
2 to 4, plus a Scorekeeper

Object
To compare the numbers on two number cubes and be the first player to score 10 points

Materials
- Shark Attack game board (page 17)
- 2 number cubes (page 18)
- Paper and pencil (for the Scorekeeper)

How to Play

1. Review the symbols for greater than (>), less than (<), and equal to (=) with players.

2. Players take turns rolling the number cubes. In each turn, a player rolls one cube first and then the second cube. Based on the numbers on the first and second cubes, the player decides in which shark to place the cubes in the order rolled.

   For example: Say a player rolls a 1 with the first number cube and a 6 with the second cube. He or she would put the 1 in the first square of the "Less Than" shark and the 6 in its second square.

3. The Scorekeeper awards a player one point for each correct placement. The first player to earn 10 points wins.

Variation:
If you want students to practice with larger numbers, white out the numbers on the cubes and fill in numbers from the tens or hundreds families before reproducing the cubes.

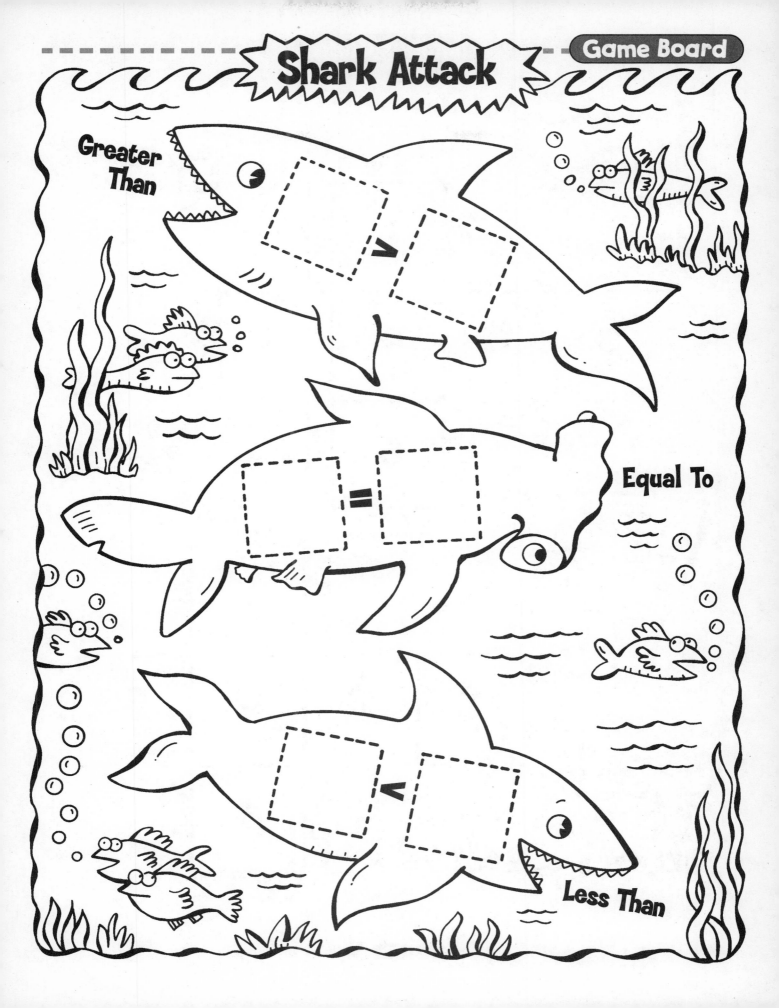

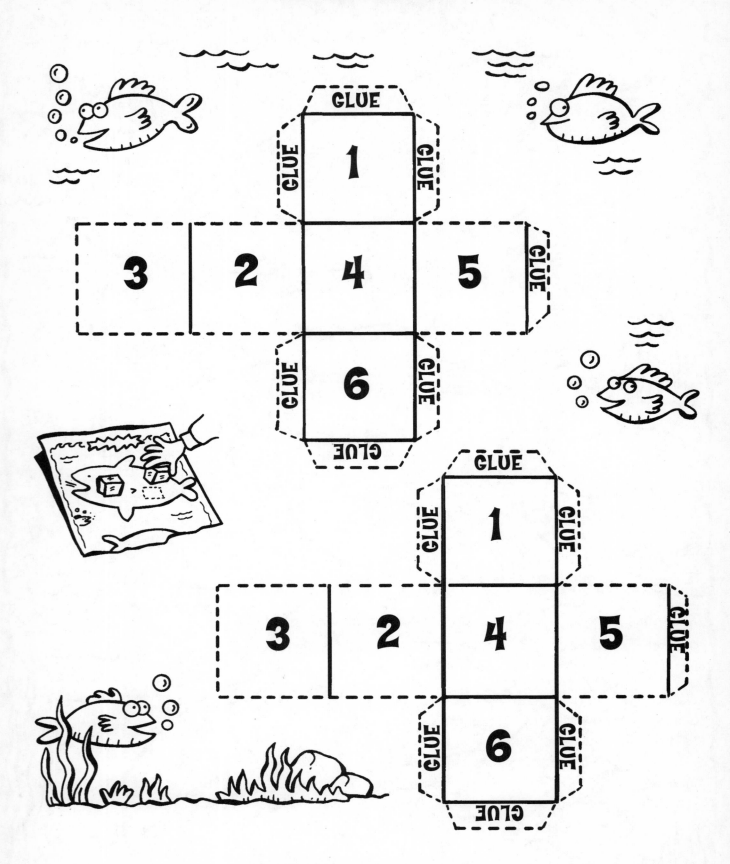

Ducks in a Row

NCTM Standard

Number and Operations

Skill

Understanding ordinal numbers

Players

2 to 4, plus a Scorekeeper

Object

To be the first player to get all his or her ducks in order from 1st to 10th

Materials

- Ducks in a Row game board (page 20)
- Number cube (page 21)
- One set of Duck cards for each player* (page 21)
- Different colored buttons (for markers)

* If young students are playing, you may wish to use only the 1st to 5th cards.

How to Play

1. Shuffle all the Duck cards and stack them facedown on the game board. Take one card out and place it face-up on the Discard space.

2. Have each player put a marker on an arrow space on the game board. Each player should start at a different space.

3. Players take turns rolling the number cube to determine how many spaces to move around the board. Each player should follow the directions on the space he or she lands on. If a player lands on a Duck space, he or she may either take a card from the pile of facedown cards or take the top card from the discard pile.

4. For a player to keep a Duck card, the card must be one that the player needs. The first card each player needs is the FIRST card, then the SECOND card, and so on. If a player draws the Duck card she needs, she places it face-up in front of her. If not, she must put the card face-up on the discard pile. The next player takes a turn.

5. The first player to collect and place all his or her Duck cards in order, from 1st to 10th, wins.

Variation:

Using two sets of Duck cards, spread the cards facedown on a table. Players take turns flipping over two cards to make a match. The player with the most matches wins.

Ducks in a Row

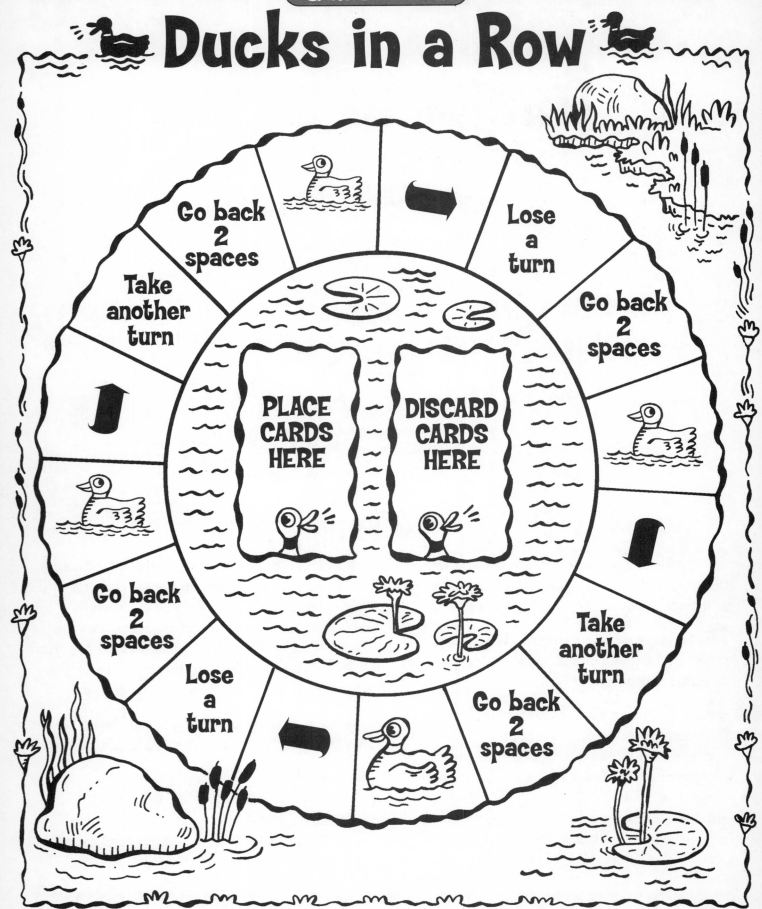

DUCK CARDS

1st First	2nd Second	3rd Third	4th Fourth	5th Fifth
6th Sixth	7th Seventh	8th Eighth	9th Ninth	10th Tenth

NUMBER CUBE

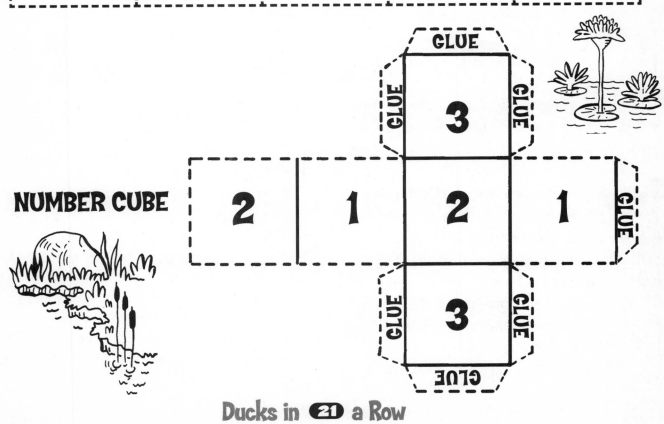

GLUE

GLUE 3 GLUE

2 1 2 1 GLUE

GLUE 3 GLUE

GLUE

Ladybug Spots

NCTM Standard
Number and Operations

Skill
Recognizing odd and even numbers

Players
2 to 4

Object
To place an odd or even number of spots on the ladybug and be the first player to cross out all the numbers on his or her Number card

Materials
- Ladybug game board (page 23)
- Odd/Even cube (page 24)
- Number card for each player (page 24)
- 10 black buttons (Ladybug Spots) • Crayon for each player

How to Play

1. Give each player a Number card and a crayon. Set the Ladybug Spots (buttons) next to the game board.

2. Players take turns rolling the Odd/Even cube to determine whether to place an odd or even number of Spots on the Ladybug game board. A player may place any number of Spots on the game board as long as it meets the criteria on the cube. The player may then cross off the number on his or her Number card, then remove the Spots from the game board.

3. The first player to cross off all the numbers on his or her Number card wins.

Variation:
To make the game more challenging, provide players with an Odd/Even cube and a 1-to-6 number cube (page 18). Place all the Spots on the game board. Have players take turns rolling both cubes. If a player rolls Odd on the Odd/Even cube and rolls an odd number with the number cube, he or she wins one Spot from the game board. The same applies if player rolls even on both cubes. Play continues until all the Spots are gone. The player with the most Spots wins.

LADYBUG

Ladybug Number Card

1	2	3	4	5
6	7	8	9	10

ODD/EVEN CUBE

GLUE
GLUE **odd** GLUE

| **odd** | **even** | **odd** | **even** | GLUE |

| GLUE **even** GLUE |
| GLUE |

Checkered Flag

NCTM Standard
Number and Operations

Skill
Sequencing numbers

Players
2

Object
To be the first player to arrange his or her Race Cars in numerical order

Materials
- Race Car cards (pages 26-27)
- Number cube (page 26)

How to Play

1. Shuffle the Race Car cards and stack them between the players.

2. Have each player draw three cards from the stack and place them facedown on the table.

3. Players take turns rolling the number cube to determine how many more Race Car cards both players should draw from the stack. Remind players to keep all their cards facedown on the table.

4. If the number cube lands on the Checkered Flag, both players turn over their cards and arrange them in numerical order from smallest to largest as quickly as they can. The first player to get all his or her Race Cars in numerical order wins. Reshuffle the cards to play the game again.

Variation:
Instead of arranging the cars from smallest to largest, have players arrange the cars from largest to smallest.

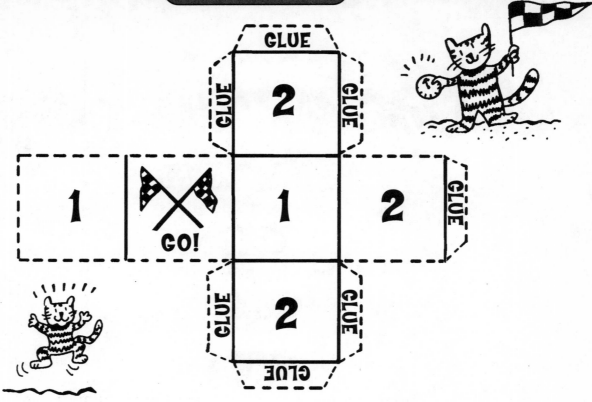

GLUE
GLUE
2
GLUE

1 | GO! | **1** | **2** | GLUE

GLUE
2
GLUE
GLUE

Race Car Cards

| 63 | 58 | 95 |
| 79 | 71 | 50 |

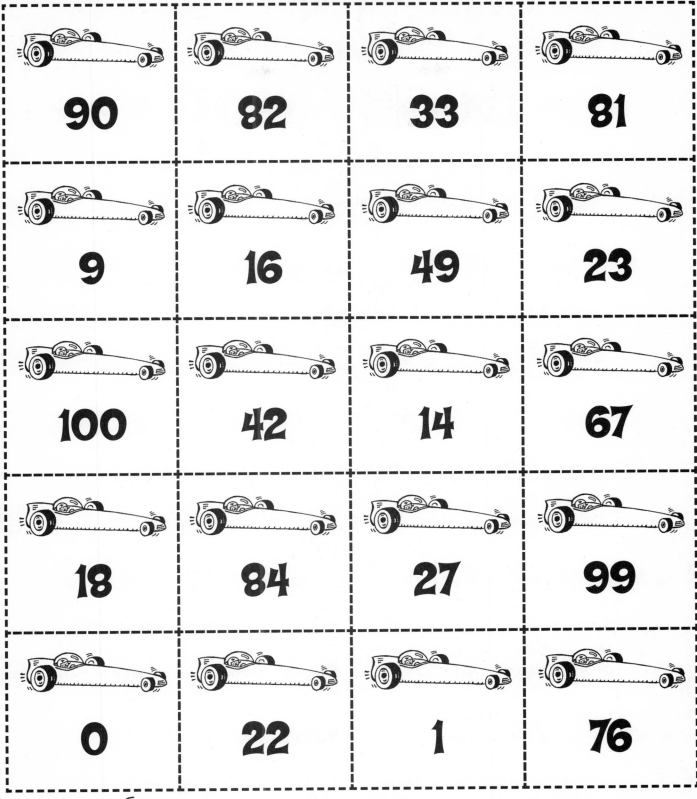

90	82	33	81
9	16	49	23
100	42	14	67
18	84	27	99
0	22	1	76

Bunny Hop

NCTM Standard

Number and Operations

Skill

Understanding relative position of whole numbers

Players

2 to 4, plus a Number Inspector

Object

To hop from one number to another on the Hundreds Chart
and collect the most Carrot cards

Materials

- Hundreds Chart game board (page 29)
- Bunny finger puppet for each player (page 29)
- Carrot game cards (page 30)

How to Play

1. Shuffle the Carrot game cards and stack them next to the game board.

2. Players take turns drawing a card from the stack for the Number Inspector to read aloud. Each player must follow the directions on the card using his or her finger puppet to hop from one number on the Hundreds Chart to another.

3. The Number Inspector checks the number on which the player lands with the answer (in parentheses) on the card. If the player lands in the correct space, the Number Inspector gives that player the card. If not, the Number Inspector places the card at the bottom of the stack.

4. Play continues until all the cards have been collected. The player with the most cards wins.

Variation:

To reinforce the concept of adding and subtracting by 10, create Carrot cards that have students hop to the numbers directly above or below the first number they start on.

Bunny Hop
Hundreds Chart

1	2	3	4	5	6	7	8	9	10
11	12	13	14	15	16	17	18	19	20
21	22	23	24	25	26	27	28	29	30
31	32	33	34	35	36	37	38	39	40
41	42	43	44	45	46	47	48	49	50
51	52	53	54	55	56	57	58	59	60
61	62	63	64	65	66	67	68	69	70
71	72	73	74	75	76	77	78	79	80
81	82	83	84	85	86	87	88	89	90
91	92	93	94	95	96	97	98	99	100

BUNNY FINGER PUPPET

GLUE

Carrot Game Cards

Start at 3.
Hop ahead 4 spaces.
Hop back 1 space.
WHERE ARE YOU?
(6)

Start at 16.
Hop back 3 spaces.
Hop ahead 5 spaces.
WHERE ARE YOU?
(18)

Start at 27.
Hop ahead 1 space.
Hop back 9 spaces.
WHERE ARE YOU?
(19)

Start at 61.
Hop ahead 10 spaces.
Hop back 1 space.
WHERE ARE YOU?
(70)

Start at 77.
Hop back 5 spaces.
Hop ahead 1 space.
WHERE ARE YOU?
(73)

Start at 38.
Hop ahead 2 spaces.
Hop back 2 spaces.
WHERE ARE YOU?
(38)

Start at 99.
Hop back 4 spaces.
Hop ahead 1 space.
WHERE ARE YOU?
(96)

Start at 55.
Hop back 4 spaces.
Hop ahead 10 spaces.
WHERE ARE YOU?
(61)

Start at 12.
Hop ahead 2 spaces.
Hop back 1 space.
WHERE ARE YOU?
(13)

Start at 62.
Hop ahead 8 spaces.
Hop back 1 space.
WHERE ARE YOU?
(69)

Start at 66.
Hop ahead 5 spaces.
Hop back 4 spaces.
WHERE ARE YOU?
(67)

Start at 23.
Hop ahead 10 spaces.
Hop back 1 space.
WHERE ARE YOU?
(32)

Start at 49.
Hop back 6 spaces.
Hop ahead 2 spaces.
WHERE ARE YOU?
(45)

Start at 7.
Hop ahead 10 spaces.
Hop back 10 spaces.
WHERE ARE YOU?
(7)

Start at 54.
Hop ahead 8 spaces.
Hop back 2 spaces.
WHERE ARE YOU?
(60)

Start at 81.
Hop ahead 10 spaces.
Hop back 10 spaces.
WHERE ARE YOU?
(81)

Start at 40.
Hop ahead 10 spaces.
Hop back 10 spaces.
WHERE ARE YOU?
(40)

Start at 10.
Hop ahead 10 spaces.
Hop back 1 space.
WHERE ARE YOU?
(19)

Start at 100.
Hop back 5 spaces.
Hop ahead 1 space.
WHERE ARE YOU?
(96)

Start at 83.
Hop back 2 spaces.
Hop ahead 10 spaces.
WHERE ARE YOU?
(91)

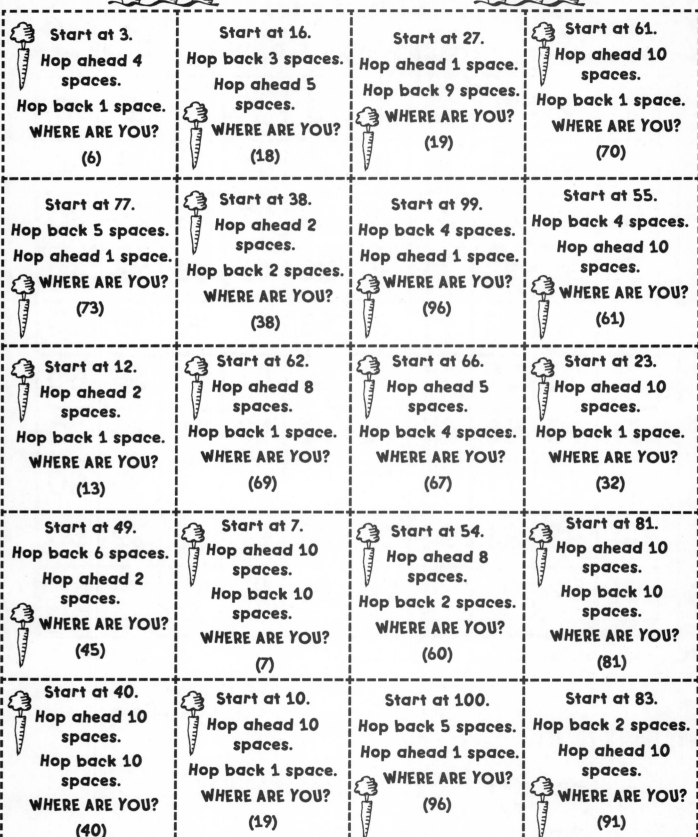

Bunny 30 Hop

Dino Dig

NCTM Standard

Measurement

Skill

Measuring using standard units (inch and half inch)

Players

2 to 4, plus a Tooth Inspector

Object

To measure dinosaur teeth and collect the most Teeth cards

Materials

- Dino Dig game board (page 32)
- Dino Tooth cards (page 33)
- Answer Key for the Tooth Inspector (page 31)
- Number cube (page 21)
- Different colored buttons (for markers) • Ruler

How to Play

1. Place the Dino Tooth cards at the center of the game board. Have each player choose a marker and place it on a START space. Each player should begin on a different space.

2. Players take turns rolling the number cube to determine how many spaces to move around the game board. Players should follow directions on the space they land on.

3. If a player lands on DIG!, he or she picks a Dino Tooth card. The player uses the ruler to measure the tooth (measure the straight line along the bottom of the card) and says the tooth's length in inches.

4. The Tooth Inspector compares the player's answer to the Answer Key. If the player measured correctly, he or she may keep the card. If not, he or she returns it.

5. Play continues until all of the Tooth cards have been taken. The player with the most cards wins.

ANSWER KEY:

Albertosaurus — 2 in.	Carcharodontosaurus — 2 1/2 in.	Spinosaurus — 5 in.
Allosaurus — 1/2 in.	Carcharodontosaurus saharias — 3 1/2 in.	Spinosaurus aegyptiacus — 1 1/2 in.
Carcharocle megalodon — 4 1/2 in.	Daspletosaur — 3 in.	Tyrannosaurus rex — 6 in.
	Nannotyrannus lancensis — 1 in.	Velociraptor — 1 in.

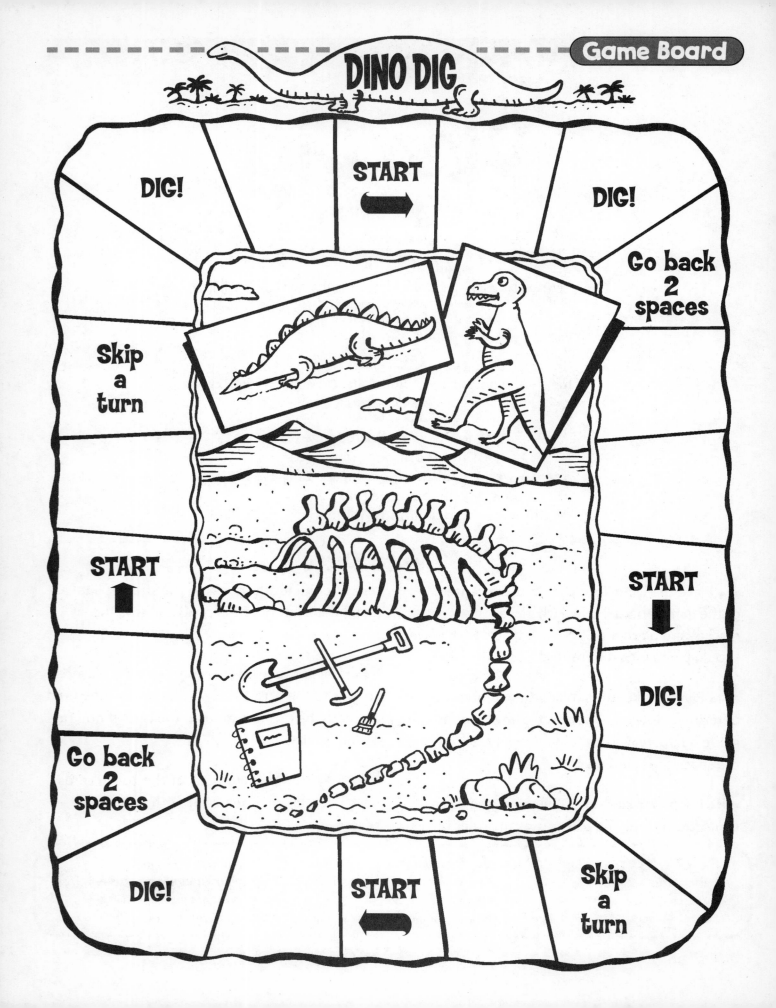

Dino Tooth Cards

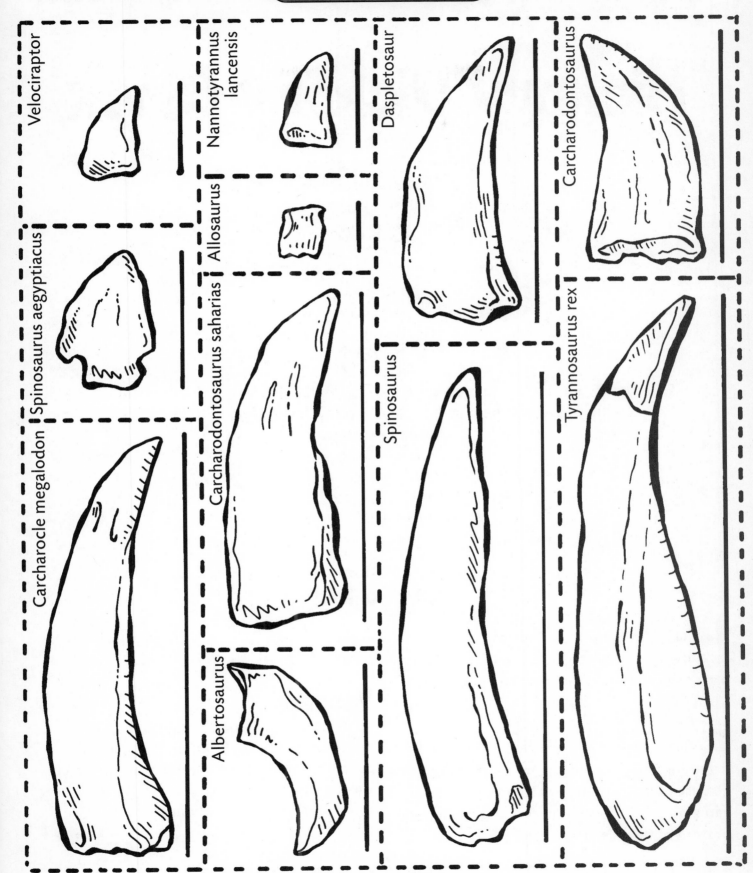

Velociraptor

Nannotyrannus lancensis

Daspletosaur

Carcharodontosaurus

Spinosaurus aegyptiacus

Allosaurus

Carcharocle megalodon

Carcharodontosaurus saharias

Spinosaurus

Tyrannosaurus rex

Albertosaurus

Dino 33 Dig

Hickory Dickory Clock

NCTM Standard

Measurement

Skill

Recognizing attributes of time

Players

2 to 4

Object

To match the analog time on the Time card with the digital time on the game board and be the first player to reach the clock (FINISH)

Materials

- Hickory Dickory Clock game board (page 35)
- Time cards (page 36)
- Mouse markers (page 36)

How to Play

1. Shuffle and stack the Time cards facedown next to the game board. Have each player select a Mouse marker and place it on START.

2. Players take turns drawing a Time card from the stack and moving forward to the nearest square with the matching time on the game board. Players put back the card on the bottom of the pile after each move.

3. The first player to reach the clock (FINISH) wins.

Variation:

To make the game more challenging, white out the times listed on the board and substitute time to the quarter hour or time to the minute. Then make a new set of Time cards to match the new board.

Hickory Dickory Clock

START

| 12:30 | 4:00 | 6:00 | 9:30 | 2:00 | 3:30 |

| 4:00 | 12:30 | 3:30 | 2:00 | 9:30 | 6:00 | 4:00 |

| 6:00 | | | | | | 12:30 |

| 9:30 | | | | | | |

| 2:00 | 3:30 | 12:30 | 4:00 | 6:00 | 9:30 | 2:00 |

| | | | | | | 12:30 |

| FINISH 4:00 | 12:30 | 9:30 | 2:00 | 3:30 | 6:00 |

MOUSE MARKERS

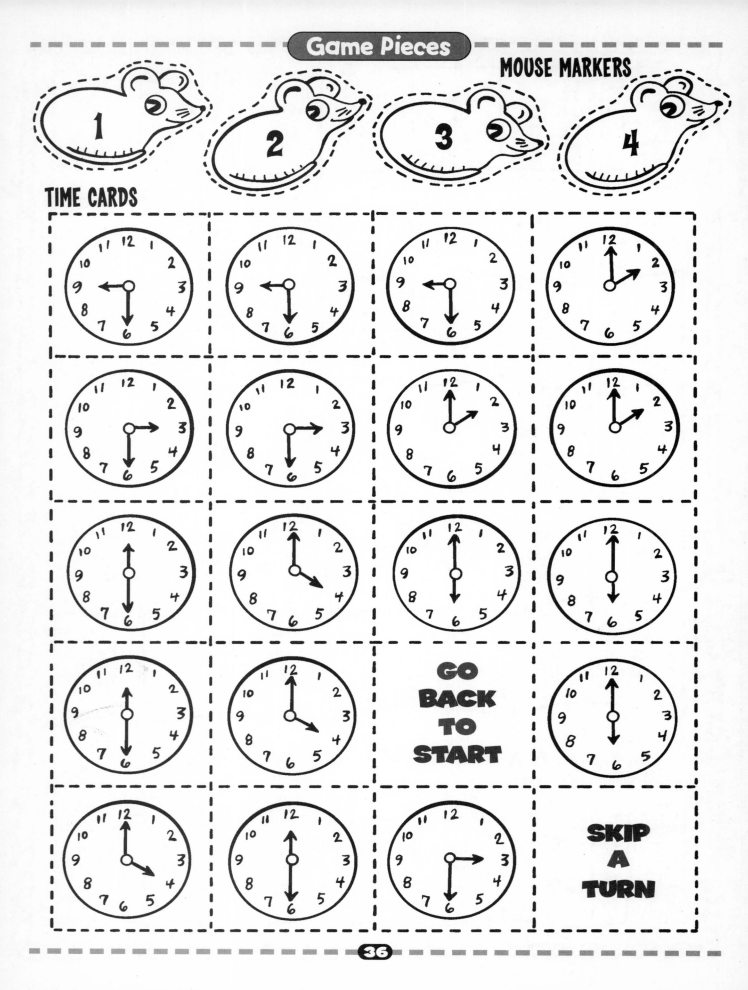

TIME CARDS

GO BACK TO START

SKIP A TURN

Pocket Change

NCTM Standard

Number and Operations

Skill

Counting money

Players

2 to 4, plus a Banker

Object

To count the correct change for each Money card and be the first player
to color all the coins on his or her Piggy Bank card

Materials

- Piggy Bank card for each player (page 38)
- Money cards (page 38-39)
- Crayon for each player
- Play money* (quarters, dimes, nickels, and pennies)

* If you don't have play money, draw coins on paper and cut them out.

How to Play

1. Shuffle the Money cards and stack them between the players. Place the play money near the stack.

2. Players take turns drawing a Money card and using the coins to make the amount shown on the card. Players may use any combination of coins, but should label each coin they are using.

   For example: If a player draws a 35¢ card, he can say, "To make 35¢, I'll use one quarter and one dime."

3. The Banker checks to see if the amount is correct. If the player is correct, he or she may color in a coin on his or her Piggy Bank card.

4. Play continues until one player has colored in all the coins on his or her Piggy Bank card. That player is the winner.

Variation:

To make the game more challenging, have players make the amounts using a certain number of coins. For example, a player may have to show 25¢ using three coins (two dimes and one nickel).

Piggy Bank Card

Money Cards

1¢	5¢	10¢	15¢
20¢	25¢	30¢	35¢
50¢	75¢	40¢	45¢
55¢	60¢	65¢	70¢

80¢	90¢	85¢	95¢
$1.00	16¢	27¢	32¢
46¢	12¢	8¢	24¢
64¢	51¢	76¢	66¢
81¢	3¢	11¢	49¢
78¢	41¢	88¢	99¢
52¢	61¢	86¢	19¢
28¢	9¢	57¢	4¢

Busy Bee

NCTM Standard
Number and Operations

Skill
Adding whole numbers

Players
2 to 4

Object
To match an addition fact with its correct sum and be the first "bee"
to reach the hive (FINISH)

Materials

- Busy Bee game board (page 41)
- Addition Fact cards (page 42)
- Bee markers (page 42)

How to Play

1. Shuffle the Addition Fact cards and stack them next to the game board.

2. Each player selects a Bee marker and places it on the START space.

3. Players take turns drawing Addition Fact cards from the stack and moving their markers forward to the nearest space that has the correct sum. Players put the card on a discard pile after each turn.*

4. The first player to reach the hive (FINISH) wins.

Variation:

Challenge students to create more Addition Fact cards to use with the game.

* If players run out of cards before they finish the game, they can reshuffle and reuse the cards on the discard pile.

Busy Bee

START

8

10

6

5

9

7

8

4

10

9

4

7

6

5

FINISH

BEE MARKERS

ADDITION FACT CARDS

8 +2	6 +4	5 +5	7 +2
4 +5	3 +6	4 +4	3 +5
6 +2	6 +1	3 +4	2 +5
4 +2	5 +1	3 +3	3 +2
4 +1	5 +0	2 +2	4 +0

Pizza Bingo

NCTM Standard
Number and Operations

Skill
Subtracting whole numbers

Players
2 to 4, plus a Number Caller

Object
To match a subtraction fact with the correct difference and
be the first player to cover all the circles on his or her "pizza"

Materials
- Pizza Bingo card for each player (page 44)
- Subtraction Fact cards (page 45)
- Answer Key (page 43)
- 8 buttons for each player (Pepperoni markers)

How to Play

1. Write any numbers from 0 to 10 inside the circles on each player's Pizza Bingo card.

2. Shuffle the Subtraction Fact cards and stack them next to the Number Caller. Give each player a Pizza and eight Pepperoni markers (buttons).

3. The Number Caller draws a Subtraction Fact card from the stack and reads it aloud. Players should cover the answer on their Pizza with a Pepperoni. The Number Caller then places the

card on the matching space on the Answer Key.

4. The first player to cover all the circles on the card correctly and yell "Pizza" wins. The Number Caller uses the Answer Key to check if that player's covered numbers are correct.

Variation:
To make the game more challenging, create new cards with basic multiplication facts (for example, 2s, 5s, or 10s).

ANSWER KEY:

0	1	2	3	4	5	6	7	8	9	10

Pizza Bingo

10 - 10	3 - 3	7 - 6	5 - 4
7 - 5	9 - 7	8 - 6	3 - 0
5 - 2	6 - 3	8 - 4	6 - 2
7 - 3	7 - 2	9 - 4	10 - 5
6 - 0	8 - 2	8 - 1	9 - 2
10 - 2	9 - 1	10 - 1	10 - 0

Piece of Cake

NCTM Standard

Number and Operations

Skill

Understanding and representing fractions

Players

2 to 4

Object

To show the correct fractions using slices of the cake and collect the most birthday candles

Materials

- Piece of Cake game board (page 47)
- Cake Slices (page 48)
- Number cube (page 21)
- Different colored buttons (for markers)
- 10 birthday candles (or buttons)

How to Play

1. Place the Cake Slices next to the Piece of Cake game board.

2. Each player selects a marker and places it on a START space. Each player should begin at a different space.

3. Players take turns rolling the number cube to determine how many spaces to move clockwise around the board. If a player lands on a space with a fraction, he or she must place Cake Slices in the middle of the board to show that fraction.

   For example: If a player lands on 2/3, he or she can show the fraction by placing two 1/3 Cake Slices in the middle of the board.

4. Each time a player shows a correct fraction, he or she gets one birthday candle. Remove the Cake Slices from the board after each turn so other players can use them.

5. Play continues until all the birthday candles are gone. The player with the most candles wins.

Variation:

Reproduce enough cake slices to make one whole cake for each player. Put all the slices face-up in the middle of a table. When you make a signal, players take slices and trade them in order to make one whole cake. The first player to make a whole cake wins.

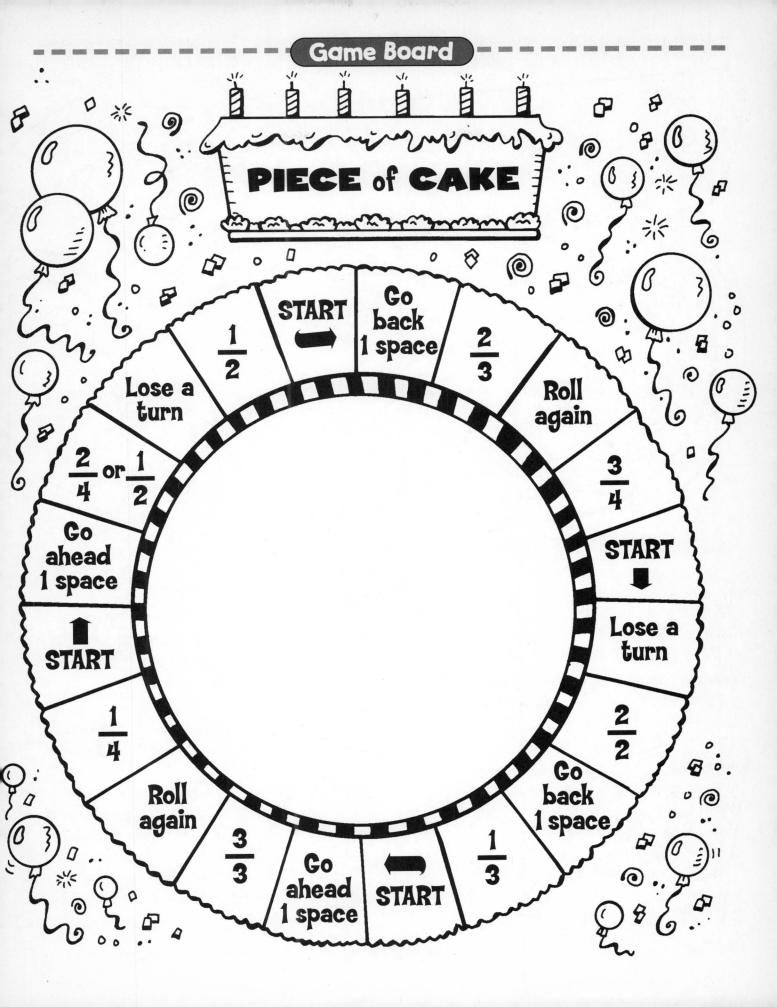

PIECE of CAKE

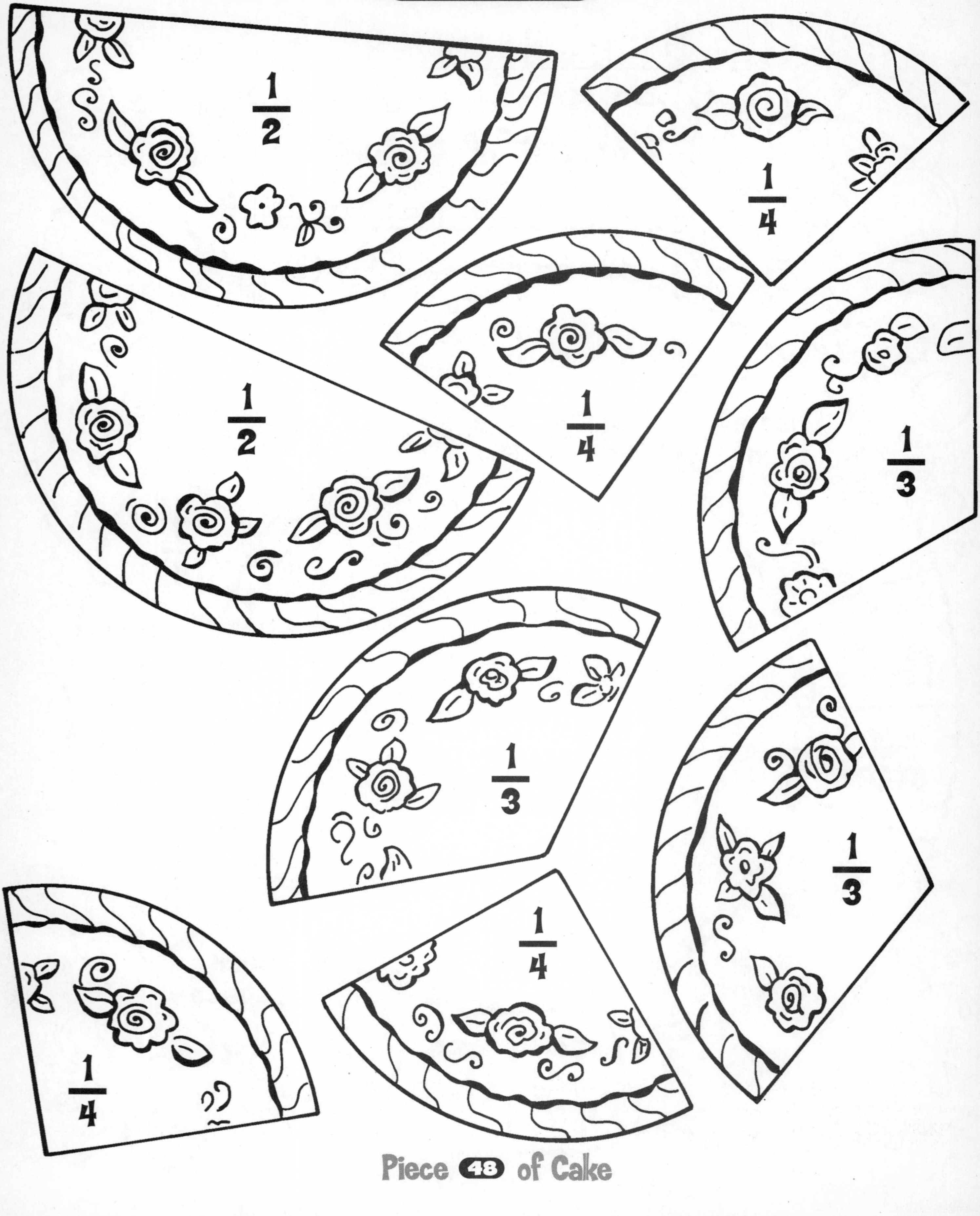

$\frac{1}{2}$

$\frac{1}{4}$

$\frac{1}{2}$

$\frac{1}{4}$

$\frac{1}{3}$

$\frac{1}{3}$

$\frac{1}{3}$

$\frac{1}{4}$

$\frac{1}{4}$